BASEBALL TALK
FOR BEGINNERS

BASEBALL

TALK FOR BEGINNERS

written and illustrated by

Joe Archibald

JULIAN MESSNER
NEW YORK

Published simultaneously in the United States and Canada by
Julian Messner, a division of Simon & Schuster, Inc.,
1 West 39 Street, New York, N.Y. 10018. All rights reserved.

Printed in the United States of America

SBN 671-32065-3 Trade
    671-32066-1 MCE

Library of Congress Catalog Card No. 69-12114

Text and Cover Designed by Michael G. Ferst

Also by Joe Archibald

BASEBALL TALK
FOR BEGINNERS

A

ABOARD

Reaching first base by a hit, a base on balls, an error, or having been hit by a pitch. Also refers to runners already on base.

ACE

The best pitcher on a team.

ALL-STAR GAME

A game played every year between the National League and the American League. The teams are chosen by the players of both leagues. Part of the proceeds goes to the baseball players' pension fund.

AMERICAN LEAGUE *See* league; nicknames.

APPEAL

An act of a fielder who claims a rule has been broken by the opposing team.

AROUND THE HORN

You are playing third base. The other team has a runner on first base. A ground ball is hit at you. You grab it and throw to second to put out the runner from first. The second baseman then throws to first base to get the batter out. It is a double play around the horn, the longest way around, so called because before the Panama Canal was built, sailing ships had to go around Cape Horn at the southern tip of South America to get from New York to San Francisco.

ASSIST

Any player who helps in a play but does not make the putout himself gets credit for an assist. He either throws or deflects the ball to another player who makes the out.

AT BAT

A player's turn to hit.

AUTOMATIC STRIKE

While you are up at bat, the pitcher has thrown three balls and no strikes. Now your manager will tell you not to swing at the next pitch because you have a chance to get a base on balls. Knowing you won't swing, the pitcher almost always gets the ball over for the automatic strike.

B

BACKSTOP

The catcher on a ball team. It is also the screen set up back of home plate to stop foul balls from hitting people in the stands watching the game.

BAG *See* base.

BAIL OUT

This is what you should do if a pitched ball comes in too close to you. It is jumping back from the plate in a hurry to avoid being hit.

BALK

If you are a pitcher, do not bluff a throw to first base if you are standing on the pitching rubber. Do not change your mind about a pitch just as you are about to throw, because it will break your delivery. Do not let the ball slip out of your glove when your foot is on the pitching slab. Do not fail to come to a complete stop when bringing your hands down from your stretch. These are balks, and the umpire will allow a man or men on base to advance one base.

BALL

A pitch that misses the strike zone at home plate and is not struck at by the batter. Four balls entitle the batter to first base. It is also the sphere which is used to play the game of baseball. Also known as apple, horsehide, pea, pill.

BALTIMORE CHOP

This is not found in a butcher shop. It is a ball hit just out in front of home plate that bounces very high into the air. Infielders have to stand by and wait for it to come down. By the time it does come down, the batter has usually reached first base.

BANJO HITTER

If you almost always hit singles or fly balls just out of reach of the infielders, you will be called a banjo hitter because you hit the ball lightly, like strumming a banjo. One of the greatest banjo hitters was Nellie Fox, who played for the Chicago White Sox and Houston Astros.

BASE

There are four bases, each of which must be touched by the runners in order to score a run. First, second, and third base are white canvas bags, each 15 inches square, between 3 and 5 inches thick, firmly fastened to the ground. Home base or plate is a five-sided piece of whitened rubber, also set in the ground, which looks like this:

All four bases are 90 feet apart, and have to be run in order. Also called bag, cushion, sack.

BASE LINES

Except for the partially chalked line running near first base, base lines are not marked on the field. They extend three feet on either side of an imaginary straight line between any two of the bases. You must keep within this area when running the bases, or you will be called out.

BASE ON BALLS

When the batter is allowed to go to first base after the pitcher has thrown four bad pitches over the plate. Also known as a free pass. Babe Ruth holds the all-time record for getting bases on balls with 2056.

BASE PATH

The running room inside the base lines.

BASE RUNNER

A player of the team at bat who occupies one of the bases.

BASES LOADED

When there are runners on first, second, and third base. Radio and TV sports announcers say, "The ducks are on the pond." Also known as bases full.

BAT

A piece of wood, smooth and round, not more than 2¾ inches in diameter at its thickest part and not more than 42 inches long. Also called club, lumber, stick, wood.

BAT AROUND

When all nine hitters on a team have come up to bat in one inning before three outs have been made.

BATTER'S BOX

The space at home plate in which the batter stands during his time at bat. It is 6 feet long and 4 feet wide, and the batter must not step outside the box while he is hitting.

BATTERY

The pitcher and catcher on a team.

BATTING AVERAGE

How good a hitter are you? To find out, divide the number of hits you make by the number of times you go to bat. If you have 5 hits in 11 times up, you are hitting .455. This is your batting average. The highest batting average in baseball history belongs to Ty Cobb, who hit .367 over a period of 24 years. He got 4191 hits out of 11,429 times at bat.

BATTING CAGE

You won't find this kind of cage in a zoo. It is used during batting practice. A three-sided fence made of metal, it is wheeled into place behind home plate to serve as a backstop and to keep foul balls from going into the stands.

BATTING ORDER

The order in which nine players on a team are to go to bat. It is made out by the manager and given to the plate umpire before the game starts. If a player bats out of turn he is out.

BATTING PRACTICE

Held before each game.

BEANBALL

A pitch that is aimed at the batter's head. If an umpire thinks such a pitch is thrown on purpose, he can put the pitcher out of the game and the league president could fine or suspend him.

BEAT IT OUT

When you hit a slow roller out in front of the plate or bunt the ball and get to first base before an infielder can throw you out. Also a ball hit in the hole at second or short can be "beat out" for a hit.

BENCH

Where team members, except pitchers, in uniform sit during a game when they are not playing on the field. It also means the team's substitutes. A manager "reaches for his bench" when he needs a better hitter or faster base runner. If a player spends most of his time on the bench, he is called a bench warmer.

BENCH JOCKEY

A player who razzes the other team from the bench. It is done mostly in fun, and the idea is to rattle the opposing pitcher or the batter up at the plate.

BLANKED *See* shutout.

BLEACHERS

The uncovered seats in the outfield. The sun always beats down there and the fans "bleach" in the sun.

BLOOPER

A short fly ball hit not too high that drops just out of reach of the infielders.

BOBBLE

Dropping the ball or letting it go through your legs. Also called an error, a muff, or a boot.

BONER

Not always called an error. It is a foolish play, like failing to touch a base while running out an extra-base hit. One of the prize boners of all time took place in the 1908 World Series between the New York Giants and Chicago Cubs. Fred Merkle, of the Giants, failed to touch second base as he was being driven home by a teammate with what should have been the winning run. Another boner is to steal a base already occupied by a base runner. Also called a bonehead play or pulling a rock.

BONUS KID OR PLAYER

What all Little Leaguers hope to be someday. It is the name for a rookie who gets a large sum of money for signing a big league contract. The biggest amount of money ever paid to a rookie went to Rick Reichhardt when he joined the Los Angeles Dodgers in 1964. It was $200,000.

BOOT

You make a boot when you drop a ball once it is in your glove or fail to stop a ground ball that comes right at you. *See also* error.

BOTTOM

The last half of an inning, when the home team is at bat.

BOX SCORE

A brief summary of a game found in newspapers and magazines that gives the position played, at bats, runs, hits, and RBI's by each player. Also included in the box score is a summary of the pitcher's performance as well as the scoring for each inning.

BOX SEATS

The expensive seats all the way down front. They are closed in and each box generally seats four to six people.

BREAK

A curve ball breaks. A base runner breaks for second when he gets the steal sign. A batter gets a break when a ground ball goes through a fielder's legs.

BREAKING PITCH

You are up at bat and a pitch comes in that looks as if it will go right over the heart of the plate. Then, just as you swing, it breaks outside or inside the corners of the plate.

BRUSHBACK PITCH

Often used against a batter who stands too close to the plate. The pitcher who throws it, they say, wants to keep the batter "honest." He knows this kind of batter often gets on base by being hit with the pitch. For example, pitchers have to keep brushing back Frank Robinson, Baltimore Orioles outfielder. Also called a duster.

BULLPEN

Where the pitchers warm up, usually alongside the right and

left field foul lines. In the newer ball parks, bullpens are placed outside the playing area, back of the outfield fences. Years ago there were big signs in many ball parks carrying a picture of a big bull and telling people to smoke a certain kind of tobacco. The signs were always placed on fences where the relief pitchers warmed up.

BUNT

Your team has a runner on first base and you're at bat. The manager orders you to bunt the ball to get the runner to second base. You slide your hands up on the bat and punch the ball, not too hard, only a few feet out from the plate and just inside the first or third base foul lines. Even if you are put out at first, the base runner generally gets to second base safely. Two of the greatest bunters in the game today are Maury Wills of the Pittsburgh Pirates, and Lou Brock of the St. Louis Cardinals. Also known as laying one down.

BUSHER

Any player who has just come up from the minor or bush leagues. It is also a name given to a major leaguer whose behavior on and off the diamond isn't as proper as it should be.

C

CALL

A decision by an umpire. The plate umpire calls a pitch a ball or a strike. Base umpires call runners safe or out, decide if a ball has been hit fair or foul, or whether a catch has been made properly.

CALLED GAME

One in which the umpire-in-chief ends play for any reason.

CATCHER

The player behind home plate who receives the pitch. He has to have strong legs, for he sits on his haunches during most of the game. And he must have a strong throwing arm. Also called backstop, receiver, the man in the iron mask.

CAUGHT LOOKING

You are at bat with two strikes against you. In comes the next pitch. It looks like a ball so you don't swing. But it was a strike and the umpire shouts, "Str-r-rike three!" You were caught looking, with your bat on your shoulder.

CELLAR

Last place in the league standings.

CENTER FIELDER *See* outfielder.

CHANGE-UP

Watch out for this pitch! It fools a lot of batters. After throwing you his fast ball, the pitcher will usually throw a slow ball with the same motion, and it can catch you off stride. Also called a slip pitch, letup, change of pace, or pulling the string.

CHECKED SWING

You start to swing at a pitch, then suddenly change your mind. If you've brought the bat more than halfway around, it's a strike. If not, it's a checked swing.

CHINESE HOME RUN

A homer that is hit into the stands just inside the right or left field foul poles, the shortest distances from home plate. In the Polo Grounds (no longer in existence) in New York City where the old Giants played, it was only 257 feet along the right field foul line. So called because Chinese coolie labor was cheap.

CHOKE HITTER

Holding the bat far up on the handle gives you the name of choke hitter. A batter does this on purpose when he wants to bunt the ball. Watch Bud Harrelson of the New York Mets at the plate. Richie Ashburn of the Philadelphia Phillies was also this type of hitter.

CIRCUS CATCH

A catch of a long fly ball that seems impossible to accomplish. An outfielder catching a ball when it seems about to drop into the stands, or when he bounces off the outfield fence, or almost "climbs" a wall.

CLEANUP HITTER

The player who bats fourth, usually the best hitter on the team, who can be relied on to drive in the runners ahead of him and so clean up the bases. Some managers today are batting their best hitters third, for they believe in that way the players will get more turns at bat.

CLOSE CALL

An "out" or "safe" call by an umpire that could have gone either way.

CLUB

Baseball team. Also refers to the baseball bat.

CLUTCH HITTER

A player who can be counted on to hit in important or tight situations is said to be hitting in the clutch. A pitcher who strikes a batter out when the bases are full is a clutch pitcher. Both are also known as a money player.

COACH

An assistant to the manager. One stands in the coach's box off first base, another in the one off third. They relay the manager's signals to the players and direct the base runners. Since they are former ballplayers, they also instruct in hitting, pitching and fielding. However, pitching and batting coaches do not usually coach from either box during a game.

COLLAR

What you will wear if you go through a whole game without making a hit. Ballplayers also call it "being horse-collared."

COMMISSIONER

The man elected by baseball owners and given complete authority over all baseball clubs and leagues. He has the power to settle all disputes between owners and players, to judge the conduct of all persons connected with the game of baseball. The first commissioner, Judge Kenesaw Mountain Landis, was elected in 1921 and served until his death in 1944.

CONTRACT

The legal paper all professional ballplayers sign with baseball clubs. When a player signs, he "inks" his contract.

CONTROL

A pitcher has this if he allows very few bases on balls and can put the ball over the plate just where he wants it to go. Sandy Koufax of the Los Angeles Dodgers was one of the greatest control pitchers.

COUNT

The number of balls and strikes called on a batter by the plate umpire. A full count is three balls and two strikes. In giving the count on a batter, the balls always come first, followed by the strikes.

COUSIN

A batter calls a pitcher "cousin" when he finds him easy to hit. Pitchers call a hitter by the same name when they have no trouble getting him out.

CROSSFIRE *See* sidearm.

CURVE

A pitch every pitcher has to have to go along with his fast ball. Thrown by a snap of the wrist, it breaks from right to left when thrown by a right-hander, and just the other way when thrown by a left-hander. The ball is gripped tightly by the middle finger, and the ball must go over the forefinger. The more the wrist is bent, the more the ball curves. The first pitcher ever to throw a curve was William "Candy" Cummings, who pitched for Cincinnati in 1867.

CUSHION *See* base.

CUT

A swing that the batter takes at a pitch.

CUTDOWN DATE

This is the time when rookies with the big league clubs "shake in their shoes." There are two cutdown dates: (1) when spring training is over and the ball clubs move north to begin the pennant race, to 27 players; (2) thirty days after the season begins, to 25.

CUTOFF PLAY

You are playing second base. The other team has a runner on first and their best hitter is up. He hits a line drive down the right field line where your right fielder picks the ball up on the run. While the base runner is streaking around the bases, you go into short right field and take the throw-in. Quickly you throw or relay it to home plate to cut off a run.

CY YOUNG AWARD

Given each year to the "Pitcher of the Year" in the major leagues by the Baseball Writers Association of America.

D

DEAD BALL

A ball is considered dead when it creates a situation where play is temporarily stopped. If a batted ball is touched by a fan, hits a base runner or an umpire, it is considered dead. It is also dead if a fielder is unable to handle the ball due to an obstruction on the playing field. Decisions on dead balls are made by the umpires.

DECKED

Knocked down by a pitch without being hit by the ball.

DELIVERY

A pitcher's style of pitching.

DIAMOND

The whole playing area.

DIG IN

What a batter does at the plate. He digs his spikes into the dirt to make sure he'll get a good swing at a pitch. Also called a toe hold.

DISABLED LIST

A player is placed on this list when an injury puts him out of the game for at least ten days. The club can then bring up a player from the minors to take his place.

DISH *See* plate.

STAN MUSIAL

DOUBLE

A two-base hit. Tris Speaker, who played 22 years for the Boston Red Sox, set the American League mark for most doubles with 793. Stan Musial of the St. Louis Cardinals holds the National League record with 725. Also called a two-bagger.

DOUBLEHEADER

Two games played one after the other on the same day. Also known as a twin bill.

DOUBLE PLAY

Putting out two men on the same play. There are several ways this can be done, but most often it occurs when there is a base runner on first. A ground ball is hit to the third baseman, second baseman, or shortstop. Unless an error is made, the base runner on first is forced out at second by the infielder's throw to that base, and the throw from the man covering second beats the batter running to first. During the early 1900's there was a famous trio of double-play makers that are talked about even today. They were Joe Tinker, shortstop, Johnny Evers, second baseman, and Frank Chance, first baseman, of the Chicago Cubs—Tinker to Evers to Chance.

DOWN THE MIDDLE

A pitch—a fast ball—that comes right over the middle of the plate.

DRAFT

To select. In baseball, drafting takes place in two ways. One occurs when a new ball club is added to a league. To make up its team, a club can choose certain players from all the other teams in that league. The second way is the free agent draft. A player who has been released by a club is free to sign a contract with any other club.

DRAG BUNT

One that is "pushed by" the pitcher, usually by a fast runner. More often than not it is good for a hit, for the infielders are not set for it.

DUGOUT

The place where the bench is located. It is called a dugout because part of it is below ground level. *See* bench.

DUSTER *See* brushback pitch.

E

EARNED RUN

Scored as a result of clean hits and/or bases on balls. A pitcher is held responsible for an earned run. An unearned run scored because of fielding errors is not charged to the pitcher.

EARNED RUN AVERAGE (ERA)

A way of figuring how good or bad a pitcher is. You find it out by dividing the number of innings pitched by 9. Then divide that into the number of earned runs. For example, a pitcher who has a record of 54 innings pitched and 12 earned runs has an ERA of 2.00.

EDGE

To beat the other team by only one run.

ERROR

Occurs when a fielder makes a mistake in throwing or catching. Also called boot.

EXHIBITION GAME

A baseball game that does not count in the standing of the teams. Usually takes place during spring training.

EXTRA-BASE HIT

A hit that allows a batter to get more than one base: two bases (double), three bases (triple), a home run. Stan Musial of the St. Louis Cardinals hit 1377 extra-base hits to set a National League record. Babe Ruth slugged out more than any other player in the American League, 1356.

EXTRA INNINGS

If a game is tied at the end of the regulation nine innings, extra innings have to be played until one team leads at the end of a completed inning.

F

FADEAWAY

Now known as a screwball. The fadeaway was made famous by Christy Mathewson, New York Giants pitcher from 1900 to 1916. *See also* screwball.

FAIR BALL

A batted ball that lands anywhere inside the foul lines.

FAN

To strike out swinging. It is also a person who roots for his favorite team. The term comes from the word FANatic.

FARM CLUB OR SYSTEM

A minor league team or teams owned by a major league ball club where young players are trained.

FAT PITCH

One that comes in over the plate about letter high and doesn't break. It is the kind easy to hit—usually out of the ball park for a home run.

FARM CLUB

FIELD

To stop, catch and throw a ball. Also that part of the ground on which a team plays.

FIELDER'S CHOICE

You are playing third base or shortstop. The other team has a runner on first. The ball is hit to you. Have you a chance to get the runner going to second? No. So you throw to first and get the batter out. The runner has reached second on a fielder's choice. The batter is charged with an official time at bat, but he is not credited with a sacrifice for moving the runner to second.

FINE

A sum of money a player must pay for disobeying a certain rule.

FIRE

To throw the ball hard to a batter or baseman. Also, what owners of a ball club do to a manager who always has his team far down in the standings.

FIRE BALL

A pitcher's fastest delivery. One with "smoke" on it.

FIREMAN

A pitcher called in from the bullpen to take over the mound for the starting pitcher when the opposing team is making too many hits and runs. *See also* relief pitcher.

FIRST BASE

The base to which the batter runs first.

FIRST DIVISION

The first five teams with the best games won and lost record in a ten-team league.

FLY BALL

A ball hit high in the air, usually caught by an outfielder.

FLY OUT

A ball caught by a fielder before it touches the ground.

FOOT IN THE BUCKET

A way a batter stands at the plate. It is considered all wrong. Instead of pointing his front foot toward the pitcher, it is drawn back toward the dugout. The expression comes from the old days when a water bucket was kept in the dugout. Al Simmons, of the old Philadelphia Athletics, hit with his foot in the bucket and ended up with a lifetime batting average of .334!

FORCE OUT

You are the runner on first. The next batter hits the ball to the shortstop, who fires the ball to second and the second baseman touches the bag before you get there. You have been forced. A base runner can be forced at third, when there are runners on first and second, and can be forced at home when the bases are loaded. No tag has to be made on a force out.

FORFEITED GAME

A game declared ended by the umpire-in-chief in favor of the offended team by the score of 9–0, for violation of the rules.

FORK BALL

A kind of slow ball. The pitcher holds it firmly between the second joints of the first and second fingers which are spread wide apart similar to a fork. The thumb helps to control the ball, which "floats" up to the plate.

FOUL BALL

Any ball that is hit and lands outside the foul lines. A ball tipped by the batter is a foul strike. If there are two strikes on you and you foul the next pitch back into the catcher's mitt, you foul out. If you foul off a third try for a bunt, you are also out.

FOUL LINES, FOUL POLES

The foul lines, marked in chalk, run along the first and third base sides of the diamond and end at the foul poles about three hundred feet from home plate. Batted balls hit outside the foul lines are foul balls. If a ball is hit against or inside one of the foul poles, it is a home run.

FOUL TERRITORY

That part of a baseball diamond outside the foul lines.

FOUL TIP

A batted ball that goes direct from the bat to the catcher's hands and is caught without touching the ground. Any foul tip that is caught is a strike, and the ball is in play. A foul tip that is caught on a third strike goes as a strikeout.

FOUR BAGGER *See* home run.

FREE AGENT

Any player no longer under contract. He is, therefore, free to sign with any club he chooses.

FREE PASS *See* base on balls.

FRONT OFFICE

Where the business of a ball club is run.

FULL COUNT

Three balls and two strikes on the batter.

FUNGO

During practice, the batter throws the ball a few feet up in the air, then hits it either on the ground to the infielder or on the fly to the outfielder. The bat he uses is thinner and lighter than the one in a regular game. Leo Durocher, manager of the Chicago Cubs, is considered the best fungo hitter in the game today.

G

GATE

The number of people who pay to see a ball game. The biggest crowd ever to see a big league game was 92,706, at the Los Angeles Coliseum during the 1959 World Series between the Dodgers and the Chicago White Sox.

GLOVE HAND

The hand on which the glove is worn.

GLOVEMAN

The name given to a very good fielder. John "Stuffy" McInnis, first baseman for the Philadelphia Athletics, set an all-time fielding record in 1921 with an average of .9991. Other great glovemen were Charlie Gehringer of the Detroit Tigers, and Lou Boudreau of the Cleveland Indians.

GOAT

A player blamed for the loss of a ball game by making an error or boner, usually during the World Series. Goats are not named in the regular season, for a few errors are expected during a 162-game schedule.

GOBBLE IT UP

To catch a ball, usually one hard hit on the ground.

GOOD FIELD, NO HIT

A player good in the field but weak with the bat. Years ago a Brooklyn scout, Mike Gonzales, was told to look over a rookie in Minneapolis. He sent the message back, "Good field, no hit."

GOPHER BALL

A pitch that is hit for a home run. Comes from "Go for the stands" or "Go for four bases," first used by baseball writers when Lefty Gomez pitched for the Yankees.

GO THE DISTANCE

Said of a pitcher who pitches the full nine innings.

GRAND SLAM

A home run with the bases loaded. Lou Gehrig, New York Yankee great, holds the record for grand slams with 23. Ernie Banks of the Chicago Cubs, and Jim Gentile of the Baltimore Orioles, are tied with 5 grand slams in one season.

GRANDSTAND PLAY

An easy play, usually on a long fly ball, made to look hard by the fielder who likes to hear applause from the fans.

GRAPEFRUIT LEAGUE *See* spring training.

38

GREEN LIGHT

A signal from the third base coach to a batter, telling him to hit the next pitch. This mostly happens when the count is three balls and one strike on the batter. Also when a runner rounds third and is signaled to go home.

GRIP

The way a hitter holds his bat. Some like to hold it far down on the handle; others prefer to grip it farther up on the wood.

GROUND BALL

A ball hit along the ground. Also called a grounder, roller, grass cutter.

GROUND OUT

A play which happens when your grounder is hit to an infielder and you are thrown out at first.

GROUND RULES

Since all ball parks are not built exactly alike, managers and umpires agree before a game on certain rules affecting play.

H

HALF SWING *See* checked swing.

HALL OF FAME

Former greats in the world of baseball—players, managers, umpires, and others connected with the game—are honored in the Hall of Fame, a room in the Baseball Museum at Cooperstown, New York.

HANDCUFFED

Said of an infielder who cannot handle a hard-hit ground ball, and of a batter who goes without a hit during a game.

HANDLE HIT

A ball hit off the handle of the bat, which drops out of reach of the infielder. Also called a cheap hit.

HANGS

Refers to a curve ball that seems to hang for a moment in mid-air before it breaks; one that a batter looks for and often hits out of the ball park.

40

HILL *See* mound.

HIT AND RUN

You are at bat and your team has a man on first. To avoid a double play, the runner starts for second as the ball leaves the pitcher's hand and you swing. If you do get a hit to right field, the runner almost always gets to third base.

HIT BY PITCH

The batter is given a free pass to first if he is hit by a pitch.

HIT THE DIRT

Sliding into a base, or something you had better do if a pitch comes in too close to your head.

HIT TO WRONG FIELD

A right-handed batter is expected to pull the ball to left field, and the left-handed batter to right field. When they hit it just the other way, they have hit to the wrong field.

HOLDOUT

A player who does not sign his contract immediately upon receiving it. Usually he holds out for a raise in pay.

HOLE

What a pitcher finds himself in when he has more than one runner on the bases with nobody out. A batter is in the same fix if the count is two strikes and no balls against him. Also a hit "in the hole" refers to a batted ball that just barely rolls between the shortstop and third baseman or between the first baseman and second baseman.

HOME PLATE *See* base.

HOME RUN

A long hit either within the park or out of the playing field that lets you circle the bases. Also called circuit blow, four bagger, homer, round tripper. Ballplayers call it "touching all the bases."

HOME TEAM

The team in whose ball park the game is being played.

HOP

The bounce a ground ball takes.

HOT CORNER

Third base, toward which the hardest ground balls are hit. A third baseman has to have a very strong throwing arm to get the ball across the diamond to the first baseman in time to get the batter out. Brooks Robinson of the Baltimore Orioles, and Clete Boyer of the Atlanta Braves, are said to be the two best hot-corner men in the game today.

HOT STOVE LEAGUE

Baseball talk among fans during the winter before the baseball season opens. Comes from what we call the good old days when men used to sit around pot-bellied stoves in country stores to talk about baseball and their favorite players.

HUMMER

A pitcher's fast ball. When thrown fast enough, the ball is supposed to make a humming sound.

HURLER *See* pitcher.

I

INFIELD

The diamond-shaped area within and including the three bases and home plate. The men playing first, second, third base, and shortstop are called infielders.

INFIELD FLY

If there are men on first and second, or first, second and third before two outs are made, a batter is automatically out if he lifts an easy fly ball (not a line drive or bunt) to the infield, even if a fielder drops the ball. This is to protect the base runners. The pitcher, catcher and any outfielder who stations himself in the infield on the play are considered infielders.

INFIELD HIT

A ground ball that does not reach the outfield and is beat out for a hit. Also called a scratch hit or a bleeder.

INITIAL SACK *See* sack.

INNING

When both teams have had their turn in the field and at bat

during which each of them has had three outs. Each team's time at bat is a half-inning.

INSIDE

Refers to the area between the batter and home plate. A pitch that passes over the inside tip of the plate is said to have cut the inside corner for a strike.

INTENTIONAL WALK

If first base is not occupied, a good hitter is usually given four pitches wide of the plate. A batter is also put on first base intentionally to set up a double play.

IN THE HOLE *See* hole.

IRON GLOVE

The name given to a fielder who makes more than his share of errors. Fans say he must wear an iron glove the way the ball bounces off it.

IRON MIKE

A pitching machine used in big league training camps that can throw curves and almost any pitch.

IVORY HUNTER

The term for big league scouts who tour the minors looking for young players who might be ready for the majors.

J

JAMMING

A pitcher throwing the ball in close to the batter. It is not in-tended as a brushback pitch, but to keep the batter from swing-ing properly.

JUNKMAN

A pitcher, usually a veteran who has lost his fast ball, who throws mostly slow pitches with great control. Eddie Lopat, who pitched for the Yankees, was one of the greatest junkmen of them all.

K

KEYSTONE SACK

Second base, so called because many key plays are made there. The keystone combination is made up of the shortstop and the second baseman. Teams refer to the keystone combination along with the catcher and center fielder as their strength down the middle.

KICK

A complaint to the umpire over a ball, a strike or a close play at any base.

KNUCKLE BALL

Almost like the fork ball. It is thrown with the thumb and middle finger pressing against the sides of the ball. The other fingers are bent at the first joint and rest on top of the ball.

L

LADIES DAY

A day when ladies are admitted to the ball park for much less than the regular price of admission. Occasionally there are days when they are let in free if accompanied by a husband or boy friend.

LAY ONE DOWN *See* bunt.

LEADOFF MAN

The first hitter in the batting order or the first man up in any inning. Because the leadoff man gets more turns at bat than any other player on the team, he must be a fair hitter and a fast runner. Richie Ashburn, when he played for the Philadelphia Phillies, was rated the number one leadoff man in either league.

LEAGUE

A group of baseball clubs playing each other during a pre-arranged schedule of games for the league championship. The first big or major league, the National, was formed in 1871, and the American League came 30 years later. In 1961 the American League voted to expand to ten teams. The National League increased to ten the following year. Then in 1969 each of the major leagues added two more teams: the Kansas City Royals and Seattle Pilots to the American League, and the San Diego Padres and Montreal Expos to the National League. *See also* nicknames.

LEFT FIELD *See* outfield.

LEG HITTER

A batter who runs so fast he beats out many grounders hit to the infield. Lloyd Waner of the Pittsburgh Pirates was the best leg hitter, setting the record with 198 singles in one season.

LINE DRIVE

A ball hit on a line, often not more than three feet from the ground. Also called blue dart, screamer. Ballplayers call it a frozen rope or "hanging out the clothesline."

LINEUP

The nine men chosen by the manager to start the ball game.

LIVE BALL

A ball which is in play.

LONG MAN *See* relief pitcher.

LONG STRIKE

A ball hit outside the park, foul.

LOSING PITCHER

The pitcher for the losing team. He can lose a game if he pitches only a couple of innings, and his team is behind when he is taken out and stays behind the rest of the game. However, if the team comes from behind and wins, it is said he has been "taken off the hook."

LOWER HALF

The bottom half of an inning.

LUMBER *See* bat.

M

MAGIC NUMBER

Refers to how many victories the leading team needs combined with the losses of its nearest rivals to win the pennant.

MAJOR LEAGUES

The American and National Leagues combined. Also called the big leagues, the majors.

MANAGER

A person appointed by the club to run the team on the field. Also called skipper, pilot, or bossman.

MEAL TICKET

A baseball team's leading pitcher, the man who comes through in the clutch. Years ago ballplayers had to show a meal ticket to be allowed to eat in the hotel dining rooms. Also called the stopper.

MEAT HAND

The hand not wearing the glove or mitt. The player uses his meat hand to throw the ball.

MEAT HAND

MINOR LEAGUES

The leagues below the majors—Class A, AA, and AAA leagues. Most of the players in the minors are owned by the major league ball clubs. The minors are always called the bushes by the major leaguers.

MITT

The gloves worn by the catcher and first baseman, which differ from gloves worn by the other players because the fingers are not separated.

MONKEY SUIT

A ballplayer's uniform.

MOP-UP MAN *See* relief pitcher.

MOST VALUABLE PLAYER (MVP)

One player from each of the major leagues chosen annually by the Baseball Writers Association of America.

MOUND

Where the pitcher stands. It is raised 15 inches higher than the rest of the infield. A slab of rubber is set into the mound on which the pitcher must have his foot before he throws to the batter. Also called the hill.

MOVE TO FIRST

A quick throw by the pitcher to first base to try and catch a base runner. One of the most talked about moves to first belonged to Whitey Ford when he pitched for the Yankees.

MUFF *See* bobble.

N

NATIONAL LEAGUE *See* league; nicknames.

NICKNAMES

Given to all baseball teams and many players whether in the big leagues or the minors. Real fans always call their favorite team by its nickname.

MICKEY MANTLE

NATIONAL LEAGUE		AMERICAN LEAGUE	
Atlanta	Braves	Baltimore	Orioles
Chicago	Cubs	Boston	Red Sox, Bosox
Cincinnati	Reds, Redlegs	California	Angels
Houston	Astros	Chicago	White Sox, Pale Hose
Los Angeles	Dodgers	Cleveland	Indians
Montreal	Expos	Detroit	Tigers
New York	Mets	Kansas City	Royals
Philadelphia	Phillies	Minnesota	Twins
Pittsburgh	Pirates	New York	Yankees, Bronx Bombers
San Diego	Padres	Oakland	Athletics, A's
San Francisco	Giants	Seattle	Pilots
St. Louis	Cardinals	Washington	Senators

Colorful nicknames have also been given to the players. Joe DiMaggio, the Yankee Clipper; Mickey Mantle, the Commerce Comet; Babe Ruth, Sultan of Swat, and Willie Mays, the "Say Hey" Kid, are the most famous.

NIGHT BALL
   Games played at night under the lights. This did not take place

in the major leagues until 1935. The only park where night ball is not played is Wrigley Field in Chicago.

NIGHTCAP

The second game of a doubleheader, even though it may be played in the afternoon.

NINE

A baseball team which consists of nine players.

NO-HITTER

A game in which a pitcher does not allow a hit to the other team. Several pitchers have turned in no-hitters, but Sandy Koufax, while with the Los Angeles Dodgers, set the record of four no-hitters.

O

OFF THE HOOK *See* losing pitcher.

ON DECK CIRCLE

Where a player waits his turn to come to bat. It is a circle located halfway between the plate and the dugout.

OUT

You're out if you take or miss a third strike, if you fly out or ground out to a fielder, if you're forced out or tagged out on the bases. You're out of the game if you are less than polite to the umpire.

OUTFIELD

The part of the playing area beyond the infield covered by the right, center, and left fielders, also known as the picket line.

OUT IN ORDER

When the pitcher retires three batters in a row without allowing a hit or a base on balls.

OUTSIDE

A pitch wide of the plate.

OWNERS

The individuals or corporations who own the ball teams. Also called magnates, moguls.

P

PARK

The place where major league games are played. Also called stadium.

PASSED BALL

Called when a catcher lets a pitched ball get by him that he could have stopped. No passed ball is charged against a catcher if a base runner doesn't advance a base.

PAYOFF PITCH

The pitch following a three balls and two strikes count on the batter. So called because with this pitch the batter receives his "payoff"—either a hit, a walk, or a strikeout.

PEG

A throw to any base.

PENNANT

What every manager dreams of getting. The flag given to the team winning the league championship.

57

PEPPER GAME

Practice before a real game starts, usually by the infielders, with a batter hitting or peppering sharp hard grounders to them.

PHENOM

The name for a highly praised rookie, who comes up from the minors, only to fizzle out in the long run. Comes from the word phenomenon.

PICKOFF

When a runner is caught off base, usually first base, by a quick throw from the pitcher or catcher. Left-handed pitchers are the best at doing this, for they do not have to turn their body to make the throw.

PINCH HITTER

A batter hitting for another in a tight situation late in the game where a hit is needed to score the men on base. If a left-handed batter is coming up to hit against a left-handed pitcher, the manager may call him back and send in a right-handed hitter. So called because the batter is being used "in a pinch."

PINCH RUNNER

A player who is a fast runner sent in to replace the batter who has reached base. The man taken out cannot return to the game.

PINE TAR RAG

A rag saturated with sticky pine tar applied to the bat handle which lets a batter get a firm grip.

PITCH

A ball thrown to a batter by the pitcher.

PITCHER

The player who delivers the pitch to the batter. He can be right-handed, a rightie, or left-handed, a southpaw. Also called the moundsman, twirler, hurler, flinger, tosser, or chucker.

PITCHERS' DUEL

A game in which both pitchers hold each team to a few hits and runs and which is usually decided by no more than one run.

PITCHOUT

Suppose you are the catcher, and the other team has a base runner on first. You have a hunch he is going to try to steal second so you signal for a pitchout—a pitch wide of the plate. It gives you a chance to make a quick throw to the second baseman trying to get the runner.

PIVOT FOOT

The one the pitcher has on the rubber as he delivers the ball to the plate.

PLACE HITTER

A batter who has the knack of hitting the ball just where the fielders do not happen to be. Ballplayers say that the ball "has eyes" for this kind of batter. Still called the best place hitter of all time is Willie Keeler of the Baltimore Orioles in 1897–98.

PLATE

Home base. Also called platter.

PLAYER REPRESENTATIVE

The player on a team, usually a veteran, who is named by the other members of the team to act for them when grievances against the manager or owners of the ball club arise.

PLAYOFF

When two ball teams finish the playing season tied for first place, they play a three-game series, called a playoff. The pennant goes to the team winning two out of the three. Since 1946, there have been five playoffs in the major leagues.

POP FLY

A high fly over the infield that can be easily caught. Also a pop up.

PORTSIDER

A left-handed pitcher.

PULL A ROCK: *See* boner.

PULL HITTER

A batter who can hit a ball just inside the foul lines. A right-handed batter pulls to left, the left-handed batter to right.

PULLING THE STRING *See* change-up.

Q

QUICK PITCH

A ball thrown to the plate by a pitcher almost as soon as he gets it back from the catcher. It is meant to catch the batter napping, but umpires won't allow it. They will call a balk against the pitcher if there is a runner on base. If not, a ball is called.

R

RABBIT EARS

A name ballplayers are called when they cannot take a razzing or ribbing from the opposing team.

RAIN CHECK

The ticket stub given back to you as you enter the ball park. It is good for admission to another game if the one for which you bought the ticket is rained out after less than four and a half innings are played. Do not destroy the rain check until you are sure a regulation game has been played.

RECALL

To bring back a player who has been sent to the minor leagues.

RECEIVER *See* catcher.

REGULATION GAME

A game in which there is a winner after the full nine innings or more are played. It is also considered a regulation game if only five innings have been completed and the umpire has called off the game for any reason.

RELAY *See* cutoff play.

RELIEF PITCHER

The pitcher who is brought in from the bullpen when the starting pitcher is in trouble. The "long" man is a relief pitcher who can go six or seven innings. There is also a relief pitcher called the "mop-up" man who is brought in to finish the game when his team is way ahead in the score. There have been many ace "long" relievers such as Jim Konstanty of the Philadelphia Phillies; Joe Page of the New York Yankees; and Elroy Face of the Pittsburgh Pirates. They often win more ball games than the starters. Also called a fireman.

RESIN BAG

A small sack of powder made from resin that pitchers use to keep their pitching hand dry. It is illegal to be rubbed on the ball. The sack can usually be found behind the pitcher's mound. Some batters use it instead of the sticky pine tar rag.

RETIRE

To put a man out.

RHUBARB

An argument between a player and an umpire or between rival players that often leads to fighting and to players or managers being put out of the game.

RIGHT FIELD *See* outfield.

ROCK *See* boner.

ROCK PILE

A bumpy infield where pebbles cause a ball to take a bad hop or bounce. Also a term used mostly by players in the Class A minor leagues to describe a diamond they have to play on. Small-town clubs are unable to afford a crew of groundkeepers.

ROOKIE

A player in his first year of professional baseball. The veterans keep calling him that until he has reached his second season in the majors.

ROOKIE OF THE YEAR

Award given annually to the outstanding rookie in each league.

ROUND TRIPPER *See* home run.

RUBBER

> The pitcher's plate, or slab. It is set into the pitching mound and must be touched by the pitcher's foot as he throws to the batter.

RUBBER ARM

> Any pitcher who can come in and relieve the starters, game after game. He is a workhorse who batters claim has an arm made of rubber. There have been many pitchers of this kind in baseball. One was Joe "Iron Man" McGinnity, who pitched two complete games in one day for the New York Giants. He did it three times!

RUN

> When a batter gets a hit and goes from base to base until he reaches home plate, he scores a run. The Boston Red Sox of 1953 scored 17 runs in one inning. The most runs scored in a game was in 1950 when the Red Sox beat the St. Louis Browns, 39–6. Also called a marker or score.

RUN DOWN

> To tag out a runner caught between bases.

RUNS BATTED IN (RBI)

> Runs batters dream about. The ones he drives across the plate when he hits safely with men on base. He also gets credit for an RBI if he gets a base on balls with the bases full or makes an out on a long fly to the outfield when a man is on third with less than two men out. In each of these cases, a run has to score. Hack Wilson of the Chicago Cubs still holds the record for the most RBI's during one season with 190. Jim Bottomley of the St. Louis Browns batted in 12 runs in a single game, a record that still stands. However, no man has ever topped the RBI total of Babe Ruth—2209 runs during his career.

S

SACK

First base is the initial sack and second base is the keystone sack. Third base is the hot corner. *See also* base.

SACRIFICE

A play where a batter is said to "sacrifice himself" so that he can advance a runner to another base. There are two kinds of sacrifices. One is a bunt out in front of the plate, the other a long fly ball to the outfield that scores a runner from third base when less than two men are out. Players who sacrifice are not charged with a time at bat.

SAFE

A call made by an umpire when he believes a runner gets to a base safely. He spreads his arms wide, palms of his hands close to the ground.

SAIL

A pitched ball does this at times through no fault of the pitcher. It "takes off" or "sails" and a batter should get out of the way of it in a hurry.

SANDLOT

Any open space in the city or out in the country where a group of boys gather to play baseball, using pieces of wood or rocks for bases. Sandlot baseball may soon be a thing of the past, for since the Little League was formed youngsters now play on real diamonds and wear uniforms. Some of the greatest major league stars came from the sandlots. Yogi Berra, famous New York Yankee backstop, learned his baseball on the sandlots of St. Louis, Missouri.

SAVE

You are a relief pitcher facing either the tying or leading run at the plate. If you get the batter and the side out and your team goes on to win, you get credit for a save.

SCALP

What sportswriters say the Cincinnati Reds, Cleveland Indians, or Atlanta Braves do when they beat any other team in their league. The rest of the big league clubs crush, smother, bomb, trample, slaughter, or rout the other teams when they win by more than five runs. The Pittsburgh Pirates scuttle their opponents or make them walk the plank. The Detroit Tigers claw the other teams when they win. Remember these terms to describe a team's action if you hope to be a sportswriter someday.

SCATTER ARM

A pitcher who has trouble getting the ball over the plate. Also called wild man.

SCORECARD

A printed form in the official program on which to keep a play-by-play account of the game. Also called a scoresheet.

SCORER

There is an official scorer for every big league ball game, and he generally is a baseball writer appointed by the league president.

SCORING POSITION

When a runner is on second or third base, he can score on a single to the outfield, or from third, on a long sacrifice fly.

SCOUT

A man hired by a major league ball club to look for promising rookies on the sandlots, in the colleges and minor leagues. He is often called a bird dog.

SCRATCH HIT *See* infield hit.

SCREWBALL

Just the opposite of a curve ball. It leaves the pitcher's hand between the second and third fingers and is pushed over the second finger by the thumb. Many pitching coaches today say this pitch should never be taught a youngster, for it calls for a twist of the forearm, wrist, and elbow which is contrary to the normal arm movement. Carl Hubbell of the New York Giants was considered the best screwball pitcher in the history of the game.

SECOND-GUESSER

A fan who tries to manage, or second-guess the team from his seat in the stands, by saying what should have been done after a play is over. Baseball writers are also apt to be second-guessers.

69

SEMIPRO

A ballplayer who plays for money but not in organized baseball. He plays ball in his spare time, outside of his regular job whatever it may be. Short for "semiprofessional."

SENT TO THE SHOWERS

A pitcher who is being hit hard by the other team is taken out of the ball game or is sent to the showers. Also used to describe any player being thrown out of the game by the umpires.

SEVENTH-INNING STRETCH

The inning when the fans stand up and stretch just before their favorite team's turn at bat, believing it will give the players good luck at the plate.

SHAKEOFF

The signal by a pitcher to his catcher that he doesn't want to throw the pitch the backstop calls for. Often it is a shake of the head, but it could also be a flick of his glove.

SHOESTRING CATCH

A catch made of a low line drive or a short fly ball to the outfield just as the ball is about to hit the ground. Sportswriters say he caught it "off his shoe tops."

SHORT WINDUP

What a pitcher takes when the other team has men on the bases. Runners have stolen bases on pitchers who have taken full windups, for they are almost to the base before the catcher can throw to second or third. A short windup is mostly called a stretch.

SHUTOUT

A team is shut out when it does not score a single run during a game. In 1913, Walter Johnson of the Washington Senators pitched five straight shutouts. Don Drysdale of the Los Angeles Dodgers threw six straight shutouts in 1968. Grover Cleveland Alexander of the Philadelphia Phillies pitched sixteen shutouts in 1916 for the one-season record. Also called blanked or white-washed.

SIDE

The opposing players who have been at bat during their half of an inning.

SIDEARM

A pitch thrown with the arm below shoulder level. The pitch comes to the plate "diagonally." Batters say that right-handed sidearm pitchers throw the ball in "by way of third base." Also called crossfire.

SIGNALS OR SIGNS

Movements or gestures made by a team's coaches to tell batters and base runners what they want them to do. A scratch of a coach's ear or a tip of his cap visor could tell a runner he wanted him to run with the pitch. A hitch of his belt could mean he wanted the batter to bunt the ball. The pitcher and the catcher have their own signs that determine what pitches will be thrown to a certain batter.

SINGLE

A hit that allows a batter to go to first base.

SINKER

A pitch that breaks low just about at the batter's knees when it gets to the plate.

SKIN

That part of the infield where there is no grass.

SLICE

A term borrowed from the game of golf. A batter slices a ball when he drives it to the outfield and it curves away from the fielder. Usually a slice curves foul into the stands behind first or third.

SLIDE

When you are running to get to a base ahead of a throw, you slide or hit the dirt. Some players like to slide on their stomach, but the feet-first slide is used by most ballplayers. The hook slide swings your body out of reach of the baseman's tag, even though he is waiting for you with the ball.

SLIDER

A pitch unknown ten years ago. Nearly every pitcher uses it today. It is faster than a curve and has a spin on it. Batters call it a "nickel curve."

SLUGGER

The man who hits the long balls for extra bases. Usually the third, fourth, and fifth men in the batting order.

SLUMP

What ballplayers say they are in when they fail to get a hit in a long string of games. It also happens to the whole team when it loses several games in a row, and to a pitcher who can't seem to win.

SOUTHPAW

A left-handed pitcher.

SPITBALL

A pitch that has not been allowed since 1920. By wetting a certain part of the ball, pitchers were able to make it behave in an unforeseeable way. More than a few batters in the big leagues today claim that some pitchers are still throwing the "wet ones." A new rule was made in 1968 requiring a pitcher to step off the mound if he brings his hand to his mouth. A ball is added to the count on the batter if the umpire rules that the pitcher has done so.

SPRING TRAINING

When big league ballplayers go south in the spring to get in shape for the pennant race. At this time they are said to be in the Grapefruit League, for most of the teams have their training camps where this fruit grows.

SQUEEZE PLAY

Your team has a man on third with only one out, and you have been ordered to bunt. If the runner breaks toward the plate with the pitch, it is a suicide squeeze. If he breaks away from third base *after* the ball is bunted, it is a safety squeeze. This is a play used only when a team needs a run to tie or go ahead in the late innings.

STADIUM *See* park.

STANCE

The manner in which a batter stands at the plate. Batting coaches say you should stand nearer to the rear of the batting box than the front and keep most of your weight on the rear foot. The swing of your bat must be level with the ground or you will always fly out or pop up.

STANDS

Where the fans sit.

STARTING PITCHER

The pitcher named by the manager to start the game. A ball club needs four good starters if it expects to win the pennant or finish in the first division.

STARTING ROTATION

The sequence in which a manager uses his starting pitchers.

STEAL

When a runner takes an extra base without being advanced by a hit, an error, or a base on balls. The two most famous base stealers are Ty Cobb of the Detroit Tigers, who stole 96 bases in 1915 during a 154-game schedule, and Maury Wills who, with the Los Angeles Dodgers in 1962, stole 104 bases during a 162-game schedule.

STRAWBERRY

Many times, after a hard slide into a base, ballplayers get a bruise on their skin the color of a strawberry.

STREAK

A batter hitting safely in at least fifteen games in a row is on a hitting streak. The longest hitting streak on record was set by Joe DiMaggio, great New York Yankee outfielder, in 1941. The Yankee Clipper batted safely in 56 straight games. A ball club is in a streak when it wins several games in a row.

STRETCH

This word has a number of meanings in baseball talk. It can be the pitcher's motion before making his delivery, or a batter trying to stretch a single into a double. The last three or four weeks of the pennant race are called the "stretch drive." The fans stand for the seventh inning stretch when their team comes to bat. *See also* short windup.

STRIKE

A pitch called by the umpire which is swung on by the batter and missed or if the ball passes through the strike zone and is not swung at. It is also a strike when the ball is fouled by the batter with less than two strikes on him or he bunts it foul or foul tips it. The umpire calls a strike too when the ball touches the batter as he attempts to hit it or if the ball touches the batter in flight in the strike zone.

STRIKEOUT

A batter strikes out when he has three strikes against him. Also called whiffing or fanning the batter.

STRIKE ZONE

When a pitcher throws the ball in the area between the batter's armpits and just above his knees and gets either corner of the plate, the pitch is in the strike zone.

STUFF

What pitchers have when they are pitching well. Also the different kind of pitches he is able to throw.

SUBMARINE

A pitcher's underhand throw, one of the hardest pitches to hit, for it seems to come right out of the ground. Ted Abernathy, relief pitcher for the Cincinnati Reds, is known as the best submarine pitcher in baseball today.

SUICIDE SQUEEZE *See* squeeze play.

SUN FIELD

That part of the outfield where the sun's glare makes it difficult for the fielder to play his position properly. Left field in Yankee Stadium in New York is one of the worst sun fields. Many fly balls have been lost there, in the sun.

SUSPENDED GAME

One called off but which both teams agree to play at a later date from the point where it was called off.

SUN FIELD

SWINGING LATE

Making up your mind to swing at the ball just as it lands in the catcher's mitt.

SWINGING OUT IN FRONT

Hitting at a slow ball before it gets across the plate. Also connecting with a fast pitch a little too soon and hitting it foul.

SWITCH HITTER

A batter who hits well from both sides of the plate against both southpaws and right-handers. There are several good switch hitters in the game today: Mickey Mantle of the Yankees; Jim Lefebvre and Wes Parker of Los Angeles; and Maury Wills of Pittsburgh.

76

T

TAG

Touching a base runner with the ball or with the glove holding the ball for the out. Catchers have to tag a runner with the ball, unless it is a force out at home plate when the bases are full.

TAG UP

What you must do when you're a base runner if you want to advance another base after a long fly ball is caught by an outfielder. You have to touch the base you're on with your foot before moving to the next one.

TAKE

A batter watching a good pitch go over the plate for a strike without taking a swing at it. Usually the manager orders a take when the batter has three balls and no strikes on him.

TAKE-CHARGE GUY

The player on a ball club who encourages his team members and keeps them on their toes.

TARGET

For a pitcher this is the catcher's mitt. An opposing player can be a target for the fans or the bench jockeys in the home dugout.

TARPAULIN

The covering that is stretched over the infield by the ground-keepers to keep it dry during a rainstorm.

TEE OFF

As a rule, to get a home run. You have teed off on any ball that reaches the outfield fences.

TEXAS LEAGUER

A short fly ball that falls safely between the infielders and out-fielders. In the old days the ball parks of the Texas League were small, and rookies who came up to the majors from that league called this kind of hit a Texas Leaguer.

THIRD BASE

The bag diagonally to the left of home plate. The runner could score from third on a single, a sacrifice fly, an error, a passed ball, or a balk by the pitcher. The third baseman covering the bag is the hot-corner man.

THUMBED OUT

To be expelled from the game by an umpire who gives the order with a backward sweep of his thumb. Batters are generally the victims when they protest a called strike.

TIE

A game ends in a tie when both teams have made the same number of runs after nine innings or extra innings. If a tie game is called for any reason, it is replayed at a later date.

TIME OUT

At the request of a player or his manager, the game is temporarily held up by the umpire.

TOE HOLD

To dig in at the plate or to plant your feet solidly in the dirt of the batter's box to get a full swing at the ball.

TOP HALF

The first half of an inning, when the visiting team is at bat.

TOTAL BASES

If you hit a single, triple and home run in one game, you have hit for 8 total bases. You just add 1, 3 and 4 to get that total. Stan Musial holds the record in both major leagues—6134 total bases. In 1954, Joe Adcock of the Milwaukee Braves hit four home runs and a double in one game. It added up to 18 total bases!

TRADE

A ball club giving up a player to a rival team in exchange for another. No trades can be made after June 15. But players can be bought or sold after that date.

TRIPLE

A three-base hit or three-bagger. Fewer triples are made than any other extra-base hit because the ball is not driven out of the park, and it usually takes great speed by a runner to get to third before an outfielder throws the ball back in. Not since 1912 has any major leaguer hit more than 36 triples in one season. J. O. Wilson of the Pittsburgh Pirates did the trick in that year.

TRIPLE CROWN

An award given to the major league ballplayer who turns in the highest batting average, the most runs batted in, and the most home runs of any player in the league. Carl Yastrzemski of the Boston Red Sox took the triple crown in the American League in 1968. Few players have won the triple crown since the game of baseball began.

TRIPLE PLAY

One of the rarest plays in baseball, especially if made by one player. It is putting three men out on the same play. This play cannot happen with less than two runners on the bases and nobody out. Only eight players have accomplished this feat by themselves. The most recent was made on July 30, 1968 by Ron Hansen, the Washington Senators' shortstop, in a game against the Cleveland Indians. This is how it happened. With the Indians up at bat, Dave Nelson singled. A walk to Russ Snyder advanced Nelson to second base. Joe Azcue lined to Hansen, who stepped on second to double Nelson, and then tagged Snyder coming from first base.

TWI-NIGHTER

Two games, a doubleheader, the first game starting at 6:00 P.M. and followed by the night game. For the fans, two games for the price of one.

U

UMPIRE

An official hired by the baseball commissioner's office to see that the rules are followed. He calls balls and strikes, gives the out or safe signs when plays are made at the bases. There are usually four umpires in a game—one at each of the three bases and the one at home plate who calls balls and strikes. He is the umpire in charge of the game. Also known as the arbiter, the man in blue.

UNIFORM

The ballplayer's suit. The first uniforms were worn by the New York Knickerbockers in 1849, and since that time the styles of uniforms have kept changing. The home team wears white uniforms, and the teams "on the road" wear light blue or gray. Also called flannels, spangles, or monkey suit.

UP

The team or the player whose turn it is to bat.

UP THE ALLEY

A hit that goes through the gaps between the center fielder and the right or left fielder. Almost always it rolls to the fence for a double or triple.

UTILITY MAN

A player who sits on the bench most of the time but who is called on to fill in when a regular player is taken out of the game for one reason or another.

V

VEST POCKET CATCH

To catch a fly ball with the glove close to the player's body as if in the vest pocket. Some players call it a basket catch, and it has been made famous by Willie Mays, the New York Giants' great center fielder. Unless such a catch comes natural to a young ballplayer, he should not try it.

WILLIE MAYS

W

WAIT OUT

Said of a batter trying to get a base on balls or waiting for the pitch he likes to hit. Two of the best "waiter-outs" in baseball are Maury Wills of the Pittsburgh Pirates and Ron Hunt of the San Francisco Giants.

WAIVERS

To waive means to give up the right to a ballplayer. Just before it is time for a ball club to cut down to 25 players, it may ask for waivers on a ballplayer. If the other clubs do not claim him at the waiver place of $20,000, he could find himself back in the minor leagues.

WALK

A base on balls.

WARM-UP

Practice before a game. Especially important for the starting pitcher to warm up his arm in the bullpen before going to the mound. Relief pitchers are allowed up to eight warm-up pitches after replacing the starting pitcher.

WARNING TRACK

A grassless area about the width of a running track near the outfield fence or wall. When an outfielder feels his spikes against it, he knows just how much farther he can chase a fly ball without crashing into the wall or fence.

WASTE PITCH

Thrown wide or high of the plate on purpose by a pitcher when he has a count of two strikes and no balls on the batter. He hopes the batter will swing at it.

WHEELS

A player's legs. He has either fast or slow wheels, depending on how he runs. It is said that Willie Davis, now playing for the Los Angeles Dodgers, has the fastest pair of wheels in baseball.

WHITEWASH *See* shutout.

WHIZ KIDS

The name given to the pennant-winning Philadelphia Phillies in 1950. There was not a single player on the team as old as 30 years. A prize rookie today is often called another Whiz Kid.

WILD PITCH

One thrown by the pitcher so high, so low or so wide of the plate that it cannot be handled easily by the catcher. To be called a wild pitch, there has to be at least one runner on base who advances. A pitcher is not charged with an error but is charged with a wild pitch.

WILD THROW

A throw by any player on the field that goes beyond the reach of the fielder it is aimed it, resulting in the runner or runners taking one or more bases.

WINDUP

The pitcher's motion just before he throws the ball. He takes a full windup when there are no runners on the bases, and a short windup when there are base runners on, to prevent a runner from stealing.

WINNING PITCHER

A starting pitcher must pitch at least five innings to get credit for a win. The winning pitcher can also be the reliever who throws to only one batter during the time he is on the mound. If he comes in to pitch with his team behind in the scoring and they go ahead to win, he is given the victory.

WOODPILE

The bats in the rack in a team's dugout. A man about to hit also is said to be going to the lumber.

WORLD SERIES

The dream of all major league players. The series is between the pennant-winning teams of the National and American Leagues. The winner of four out of seven games is the world's champions. The New York Yankees have been in more World Series than any other ball club, 29. Also known as the fall classic.

Y

YANK

What a manager does to his pitcher when he is being hit too hard or is giving up too many bases on balls. Also short for a Yankee ballplayer.

Z

ZIP

What a fast ball pitcher puts on the ball when he delivers it to the catcher.

About the Author-Artist

JOE ARCHIBALD has been writing since 1931, and to date has over forty books published for young people.

He started out to be an artist and studied at the Chicago Academy of Fine Arts. Then he became a reporter for Boston newspapers. Combining his writing and illustrating skills, he worked for the McClure Newspaper Syndicate as a panel artist and sports columnist, and for the United Feature Syndicate as a sports cartoonist.

During World War II he was with the American Theatre Wing, entertaining the wounded in hospitals along the Atlantic seaboard. In 1945 he went overseas as a Red Cross Field Director. Since that time his humorous chalk talks have taken him two-thirds of the way around the world. He is a member of the National Cartoonist Society, the Authors Guild, and is on the Board of Directors of the American Cancer Society, Westchester Division. His interest in community affairs was rewarded by an honorary membership in the Port Chester, New York (where he lives) Rotary Club. But despite a busy schedule, Mr. Archibald finds time to paint and exhibit water colors.